Turns & Twists

Also by James B. Nicola

poetry

Fires of Heaven:
Poems of Faith and Sense

Quickening:
Poems from Before and Beyond

Out of Nothing:
Poems of Art and Artists

Wind in the Cave

Stage to Page:
Poems from the Theater

Manhattan Plaza

non-fiction

Playing the Audience:
The Practical Guide to Live Performance

6/23/24 *To* *Whitey and Bonnie,*
Enjoy these poems —

Turns & Twists

and everything!

Poems

by James B. Nicola

James Nicola
"BRUKO"

Cyberwit.net
Allahabad, UP, India

Cover image, taken from a photograph by Rzuwig, "Krzywy Las -
Nowe Czarnowo 2," 2012. Courtesy of Wikimedia Commons,
Creative Commons License.
Back cover photograph: Eve Sonneman.

First Edition: 2022
Rs. 200/-

Cyberwit.net
HIG 45 Kaushambi Kunj, Kalindipuram
Allahabad - 211011 (U.P.) India
http://www.cyberwit.net
Tel: +(91) 9415091004
E-mail: info@cyberwit.net

Printed at VCORRE PRESS.

for my brother

who has come so far

Turns & Twists

Table of Contents

one
? ? ?

Endings 3
Riddle 1 4
Which Comes First? 6
Urban Adjustments 7
Cloud 8
You Can't Compare Apples and Oranges? 9
Sway 10
The Existence of Two 11
Math, Defender of the Faith 13
Sides 16
The Shortest Distance 18
End of the Line 19
Probability 20
product 21
Round the Corner 22
Figurative 23
Paradox 24
Coil 25
Genesis 26
Generations: An Interactive Riddle 28
This That Here There Now Then & What's Between 30
The Unseen Branch 32
V 33
Five Things that Can't be Proved 34
The Process of Sleep 36
The Gate 37
Construct 38
Doppelganger 39

Constant Companions 40
At a Mirror 41
Riddle Using *They* & *Them* 42
The Test 43
Yours? 44
Test Markets 45

two

! ! !

The Roar of Grass 49
Full Service Staff 50
Flight of Knowledge 51
Huey 53
Word Choice 55
Silk Worm 56
I met a modern man 57
Looks 59
My Pothos 60
Priestess 61
Posture 62
Achievement 63
the tamer 64
Critics 65
Horse Man 66
Sudden summer rains 67
Mad. Man 68
The Great Party 69
Forgiving 71
Blossoms 73
How You Know 74

three

. . .

The Arbitrary 79
The Ride 80

Riddle 4 81
"Made Thing" 82
Sodden Song 84
Imaginary Options 87
clothes weep in the dryer 88
Spoon and Dish 89
Look 90
Mustard 91
Hephaestus at the Forge Shows his Back Room 92
Venus and Vulcan 93
How True Love Lies 94
Proofs 96
Leap of Love 98
Condolences 2 99
even / a red tear 100
Thetis 101
Ariadne 102
Last from the Past 103
Cemetery Patterns 104
By Graveyards 105
How and Where 106
After a Calamity 108
On Turning Adversity into Art 109
Tattoo 110
Whether or Not 111
Shadows 1 112
1985 113
My Marker 114
Meeting of the Minds 115
Syzygy and Triangle 116
Authorship 117
turning 118
Balm of Innocence 120
Before Language 121
Trip of a Lifetime 122

Notes

A title *in italics* indicates an untitled poem identified by its first line or phrase.

*

The symbol

Δ

at the bottom of a page indicates a blank line between sections of a poem wherever that line is lost in pagination.

*

Multiple blank lines (as an alternative to asterisks or numerals) are intentional.

* * *

Another Note

No actual person, living or dead, should be construed as represented in these poems except where mentioned expressly by name. The verse has been hewn out of welters of experience fertilized by imagination—and vice versa.

Welcome to my world.

—JBN

Man proposes;
God disposes.

Alexander Pope

one

???

Endings

It's going to happen in a certain way,
though what it is, or what its way is, we
don't know. And those who do know will not say.
Nor do we know how many there might be
who know. I get the feeling though that they
would like to tell us, and are trying to,
to warn us, so that with an unknown wis-
dom, we might help ourselves, adjust a few
of our habits, thoughts, values. What I do
cannot prevent it—that's the way it is,
that's all—but I'll have that much less to rue,
and might, with luck, just manage to delay
it, so that I might have this time with you.

Riddle 1

The queen to whose realm we all are headed,
like it or not, though if you ask us
if we are ready for her we say, though not invariably,
No no no no no no no no No!

On her ship, we are all passengers—
likewise unwilling, mostly, and so we try
to think of ourselves as other
than abject subjects.

And for any deal in cold specie
the trust depends on the exactness
of her count. States have been felled
denying her, as businesses have come
to sudden stops.

She is the hallmark of an era,
the sign of every age,
and often lends her name to either one.
She's the enemy of permanence in the peerage
as nobility and workers moderate
between. Her promise elevates
those who brandish hope even when laced
with calamity.

Till heaven's won she carries
on a lanyard, like a housekeeper

with a chatelaine, the only key
to redemption, progression, being alive—
being.

Solution: See answer page at back of book

Which Comes First?
or,
Chicken-or-Egg Revisited

The writer stares, agape, pen poised in hand.

The unborn, eight months twenty-seven days,
toes past a verge it cannot understand.

Wild teenage boys who wend their gawking ways
from stuffing muck into their heads in class
to packing bags at local grocery stores
twelve hours a week, to descending en masse
on Friday evenings, filling the dance floors,
cafés, and movie houses with their dates,
prepare by rote for lives of work and love.

Meanwhile the genius hammers on and waits
for strokes of inspiration from above,
years given, getting ready to receive.

So we *begin* in order to *conceive*.

Urban Adjustments

When you live in the hurlburl of
a city you start not to notice
every light or horn honk or *nice day*

But you start to be impressed
or able to be impressed by the least
and overwhelmed by absolutely nothing.

2.

Don't pick the cherry from the cherry tree
until you take a sample of the soil
and have it analyzed professionally.
Nor drink the water here until you boil

and filter it, needless to say. If that's
too much, at least try not to breathe the air.
Signs here and there indicate that the rats
have been poisoned, though they don't seem to care.

The sirens of the medics and cop cars
send shivers through my scoliatic spine,
while blood and belchworks from my favorite bars
distinguish the sour stench of urban brine.

Yet still we go and drink. And in the parks
the raspberries hang low, dowsed in goose poo.
Ghosts scare my dog until he barks and barks and barks.
City living's strange when you are new.

Cloud

A downpour's omen, or of some worse grief,
But from the heat, at least a while, relief.

You Can't Compare Apples and Oranges?

Why does the rhetorician refer to
   tart apples and sweet oranges as if
their several similarities and diff'rences are something no one
can work through?

It's not so impossible to compare
   the two, not to metaphorgers like me.
It's easy as juxtaposing the sea with life, making a flower where
none is there,

or putting sounds together to suggest
   a snake: "So Seton sneers"; or a newborn:
"Ga-baba-mama"; or a blaring horn: "We-ouw-oo"; or to
compare and contrast:

   An orange is sunshine; an apple, soil.

What can't be done, the poet lives to foil.

Sway

Cows' tails sway
So flies stay out;

Wives' tales sway
So lies stay in.

The Existence of Two

The number 2 amazes me
snugly tucked twixt 1 and 3.

The sum of itself with itself, $x + x$,
or product, x times x, or
raised to its own power, x^x,
gives you the same
result, name-
ly, four.

There's no number about which this is true
other than the number 2.

This does not prove, alas, that 2 exists, so I must be
content with the limitations of 1, the imperfections of 3.

Still, whether or not they are for real
　　(I refer to 3 and 1),
they provide a yearning feel-
　　ing, complications, and even fun.

So I can trust them as if they are
　　(again, I speak of 1 and 3) —

if not as fact, as meta-four,
      if not as simile.

Yet the daft, intrepid soul suspects
the possibility of x times x
or an x that can be added to
a like x, or raised to the power of
itself, to become more real than true,
more fine than life, more fact than love,
and so prove to me the truth of 2
the day I met or shall meet you.

Math, Defender of the Faith

It wasn't that
I thought
a lot
but thought
one thing—
a dot.

Because
that meant
there was
a dot—
I thought,
less innocent.

And then I got
to thinking
and the dot,
it got
to blinking:
and with the thought
I thought I knew
I was.

Not that
I thought
and was
as Descartes thought
things through,
ergo sum

Δ

but thought
a thing—
one dot:
which meant
there might be
two:

which meant
if there were me
there might be
another me, like you.

So were it true
that nothing was,
still, in the thinking
we could be

or,
more
accurately,
become—

which even
if Rene's still winking
reassures me
some.

Do you see
a dot
too
and is your dot
blinking?

What
is that?
you're thinking
that
you do?

Amazing such a thing
or thought
as a dot
so taught
so small
takes one from naught
to everything,
from scarcely aught
to all.

Sides

There are more sides to the single square
Than the four of which I'd been aware.
For off the form lie both an *in-*
And *out-* side. Then there are two twin
Sets of points, *over* and *beneath:*
One, thought, or heaven; the other, death.
They're joined like Aristophanes'
Hermaphroditic lovers. These,

Too, can be tilted like a plate
To bias how we contemplate
The universe around a square.
A *right* side can be labeled, there;
Here, *left.* Then: *north, south, west* and *east,*
And, well—*southwest,* to say the least,
Then *south-southeast* and *west-northwest* . . . .
(I leave to you to list the rest.)

And once I'd thought I'd seen them all
I saw a side called *practical,*
Then the *impractical* one, too.
Oh, what's a counting man to do—
Do sides stretch to infinity?
You start to see the quandary
The analytic soul has faced
Ever since four had first been traced.

"How many sides to any square?"
More than we know. The question's where

The next might be for us to find:
Around the square, or in the mind?
The answer may not be a num-
ber like a product or a sum,
but lies more likely in the pause
of a stymied proof or subordinate clause
that starts with a lingering *because*—
then grows, as an awareness does.

The Shortest Distance

The shortest distance between two people
is prayer. You might have thought it should be love?

Think: horse-drawn carriages making a trip
have broken down, nags crumbled, fallen, died,
for trysts. But send prayer overseas
without even a postage stamp affixed:
you know that it arrives there instantly.

The technique works best when the expectation's
humble, but the sentiment sincere.

End of the Line

Though in theory there is none
either arrowhead has one
so any line you actually draw has two.
Each implies there's not an end
where we see one. We pretend
for math, but the fact is, for you
to make an endless line you'd have to be
Someone who can keep drawing endlessly.

You do not have that much free
time on your hands. Neither do I.
But if there's a line that's true,
there must be such a Person. Who?
Maybe He or She five shy;
maybe, the epitome
of hard persistence and humility,
and with little else to do
today, tomorrow . . . hell, eternally.

Probability

W

hen

he brought in

the board with beads

which rolled down a sort

of pyramid to study probability,

and they lined up in columns at the bottom

in an upside-down V formation like a bar graph with

the center the highest, the edges the lowest, and gave us the equation

that defined the curve of the beads, I took the thing and tilted it

the other way and said, Look, we're all headed

the same place, 100% probability.

We agreed that a life was

probably like two

tilts of the

boar

d.

product

Like a will-o'-the-wisp, the i
in math may do and glow
but not be, being a fruit of imagination.

But, like the i in poetry,
i can adjust and grow
into something by applying multiplication,

the product of itself to the power
of ^{2}, becoming real
albeit less than nothing—till it's done

again, some seaming hour:
Then our i^2s will feel
as 2 square nobodies becoming 1.

Round the Corner

Are you in the fight for the end,
or in the fight for the fight, my friend?
And are you in the fight till the end?

What about if the end came before
the fight was over? Would you relent?
If not, then what are you really fighting for?

Not only discourse, then, but all
good fights are circular, and bent.
A win or fall is, after all,

only to be risen from.
So choose to stay behind and win
if you must or, rather, choose to come
and round the corner to where we begin.

Figurative

To say one's given one hundred and one
percent—that is a mathematical
conceit (like zero, infinity, *i*,
or negatives: You can't give more than all),
a figure of the imagination
as well as speech. It's like when fools will try
to buy the Brooklyn Bridge, or leap and fly,
as these are things one cannot do or buy.

The product of two imaginary
values, albeit negative, is real,
though, therefore an account of how I feel
giving all, and more—two, two thousand, three
bazillion times more, up to infinity,
until there's less than nothing left of me.

Paradox

I just heard: *He has most who is possessed*
by least, and least possesses. I confessed
the other day to being the poorest.
The wit too subtle, you were not impressed
and I have lost—yet with the loss am blest:
I've all this time to meditate and rest
and reckon this last loss would make me just
about the poorest, therefore the richest,
if not for the compounding interest.

Coil

A snake coils into half a double-helix
like half a molecule of DNA
or half a pair of lovers. Either way

the single snake comprises only half
of the creative thing it wants to be:
a tabernacle of fertility.

And *helix*, after all, does rhyme with *felix*,
the Latin not for *snakelike*, but *happy*.
When someone with a graduate degree

goes on about Kipling, they make me laugh;
as do analyses of Genesis,
whose author wisely kept anonymous

well knowing, even then, snakes did not talk.
So, much as I love Kipling's mongoose, and
can empathize with Eve and Adam, banned

from Eden for all time, I will not walk
in their shoes, or bare feet, but rather slither—
in quest of Paradise, lest I wither.

Genesis

This Is Not True.
                    And yet if this is true
then
    This Is Not True,
                        which "this" clearly says.
This makes This not only false, but true too.
If false, then
            This Is Not True
                            is not true,
so rather,
        This is true,
                    which clearly says
'This Is Not True.'
                    This has me in a daze.

From This the universe got moved and wrought
as matter with anti-matter was spun
into a yarn of Something, which is why
a creature as confusion-crammed as I
won't mind pitting This against This Is Not:
Without conflict, Nothing ever gets done.
Just This Is True lies there inert and static;
breeding no force of moment or design,
it bores. The obverse is more enigmatic
and stretches a lone point into a line,
then bends This line back on its origin
making the First Circle of Paradox,

kicking the First Tick into All the clocks
so Everything can, did, and shall, begin.

Is this not true?

This is not "true":

it Is.

Generations: An Interactive Riddle
(Who are "you"?)

Your Great-Gran' was a prisoner and spent
Both day and night bound by a (double) chain.
Flies on the wall would swear he never went
Anywhere. But he didn't need a plane
To fly me to the farthest continent,
Nor liberty to lead me down the lane.

Your Gran' (a wizard too) would, in the car,
Lose all his magic powers, so I'd walk
Around with him indoors. His repertoire
Of words was not his own. That didn't shock
A single soul, though: Whose words ever are?
And flies on walls would swear he loved to talk.

Unchained but bound together, you and I
Now take each other anywhere we care
To go (and any way: We even fly
On aeroplanes as one). With ample air
There's ample magic, too, for those who buy.
Lately, though, it seems that everywhere
We go together (even in the sky),
Neither one of us is really there.

Envoi
If searching souls should find this riddle and
not print it out, nor read it on a screen
that's wider than a palm (as I have planned
for most), here's one more hint to what I mean:
As eyes peruse the problem now in hand,

"I's" also hold the answer, in between.
(If even still souls do not understand:
Solutions might be felt as well as seen.)

Solution: See answer page at back of book

This That Here There Now Then & What's Between

The There Is not
      (The Oxymoron:)
   an Infinite Nothing

but rather, Then
      (The Pleonasm:)
   a Limited Something

Between the Two
      (of There's
   a Between):

Our Ghosts
      (living and dead)
   and Glory.

Beyond . . .
      What truer name have We
   but God?

Within . . .
      What apter word
   than Hope—

That Is,
      the God
   That's Here

Δ

And Now . . .
     What finer
   Bond

than That . . .
     This . . .
   Ours?

The Unseen Branch

You've heard that philosopher's canard,
if a tree branch falls or breaks in the forest,
and no one's there to hear it or see it,
does it actually exist, did it fall, did it break?

Well I've got news. *You've* heard it!

Or are about to—
        Krackkk.
Now close your eyes and try the sound again, then open them.

You back? Did you hear it? So, that's that.

And by the way,
I've been to the forest
and seen the stick,
if you can believe that.

* * *

Of course the logistical conundrum arose:
Was the stick I saw the one the philosopher was talking about,
the one that no one saw, which it can't be, since I saw it?
Well I asked the stick,
and can report to you now
that yeah it was.

You want to see it, too?
Well all you gotta do
is close your eyes
and go to the forest.

V

Does a vee of
            t
               h
           r
         ee
or
                f
                   o
              u
            r
m
    a
      k
          e
            a
               g
                 a
                    g
                      g
                        l
                    e
                 a
              n
            y
          m
        o
      r
    e
?

Five Things that Can't be Proved

There are Five Things that can't be proved to be,
cannot be held, be measured, or be seen:
Sleep, Love, Zero-Nothing, All, and In-Between.

You can be stirred from Sleep, and you can see
sleep's effects, and can feel, under a cover,
a sleeping soul, but can't, per se, see it.

You can love the world, or just a single lover,
but cannot actually perceive, to wit,
Love.

      Nor Zero: Oh, sure, there's none of some-
thing, but, like Zero, Nothing is a thought,
not a thing. You cannot see what is not.

And you can count all of X, but can't come
within Infinity of All of All.
Such are the limitations of a soul
trapped by a mind and body.

            And of these,
though Sleep might swell, it's only Love which grows. . .
or glues the distance. . . or binds as it flows. . . .

Love is mysterious, unseen until
life is over, the Everything is Nil,
the mystery revealed: then a soul sees
Love for the first time—though we might except

a trillion lovers, and a handful of
poets, who've claimed, at least when they have slept,
to have actually seen what they call Love.
The way they talk at times, I'm loathe to doubt
them. So, between the days, I dream about
the universe's souls as teeming trees
with one ancestor, possibilities
limitless, and the xylem and phloem
as Love, flowing inside, from root to sky,
invisible until the day we die,
or, In-Between, like blood and bile, which flow
both ways—All ways—at once, take root, and grow.

Grow what? Why, a miracle . . . a soul . . . a poem.

The Process of Sleep

I went to bed with a problem last night
   which had been waggling at my brain all day.
I could only come up with two half-right
   solutions; neither one went all the way.

But I was worn and weary, so I slept,
   during which time one part of me kept working,
or must have, though I did not dream, except
   of waking this morning to coffee perking—

And it is perking. That's one dream come true.
   And now this third solution's come to me.
I test it—and it works the whole way through.
   Last night I could not, but today I see.

What Mystery that lends the dark a light,
and mornings, sometimes, such a burst of sight.

The Gate

I once saw in the middle of a field,
I mean quite in the middle of nowhere,
A gate. On one side stretched for miles the field;
The other, the same field. I came across
This gate spying it from neither direction,
Though how that can be possible, you ask
As I did. Yet it was as if the gate
Asked me, while I was hovering above
(Or buried under?) *Which side of the gate*
Do you want to be on? Then I—I woke.

You see how dreams make all things possible,
Even a third side of that nagging gate,
And its illogical recurrent query,
The daily basis on which we all live.

Construct

In front of me there stands a simple door.
    If I turn around I stand in front
    of it, which can open, but can't turn
    as I can. It stands—if a door can
    be said to open, close, hinge, and stand—
    where it is and, if my eyes are open,
    whence I perceive it. For where it is
    is a product of how I perceive
    it. I walk to it. Now it is, or
    appears to be, changed. The walking has
    dramatically changed how it appears,
    although I know it hasn't changed, not
    really, unless I touched it. I know
    I haven't. And yet it grows as I
    approach. Size is relative, and yet
    I haven't shrunk. And now what is it?
    Ajar? Have I touched it? I haven't.
    I am surprised the door is ajar
    now. In any event, I am surprisingly
    touching it to walk through now as you
    once, days-months-years ago, walked through it,
    and begin my remaining days in
    the other half of the world—begin,
beyond this simple door, another world.

Doppelganger

Did you want me, or my doppelganger?
Oh, you have a doppelganger, too?
That, then, would explain the sudden anger
and why I wasn't sure that you were you.

Is yours dark and heavy but so subtle
that you barely notice when it's there?
Have you ever faced it to do battle?
Have you ever tried to find a cure?

The thing with mine is this: I often find that
it hears what I can't hear and it can see
what I'm blind to. So I hope you don't mind that
it tags along with you and you and me.

Constant Companions

And I see two of you just as there are
two of me, sometimes three or four or more

each one the same yet not quite. The image
not imaginary, not from magic,

not the plaything of a lonesome child
or lunatic whose thoughts are running wild,

nor giant rabbit in a Broadway play—
but a companion, who in every way

possible is as constant as the sea.
The hope of a future! Who might you be?

Who might I, who am but the germ, the seed
of someone better? All right, if you need

a bolder metaphor, the answer's clearer
over here. Come and look into the mirror.

At a Mirror

When I'd turn to him, he wouldn't turn away.
So I decided: Why not trust him, why
not talk to him? He seemed a little shy,
a little brazen, I can't really say.
But he could look directly in my eyes,
not flinching, and appeared content to stay
as long as needed. Now how many guys
have you known like that? Too few, right? One day

I had a secret to confide. I drew
a little nearer, ready to start in,
but at the same time he came toward me too.
And so I waited for him to begin
until a mist between rose suddenly
as breath, dissolving him, absolving me.

Riddle Using *They* & *Them* as so-called "Non-Binary" Personal Pronouns with Singular Meaning while Taking a Plural Verb

I cannot do without them any more than I could do without
    you
yet I could do without them if I chose to.
They're like a lover sought but holding back:
I cannot hate them. How I wish I could.
They reside in my apartment
enjoying an infernal sinecure
but don't mind being kept under foot:
They will not leave me until I let them go.
In other words, they are not fickle.
What's more, they do not interrupt
but only elate or disappoint.
They do not love, they cannot, but only
help me love myself
or hate myself.
They are not fair, but cannot be dishonest.
I cannot stand them, but I stand upon them
and stand by what they say to me, unless I lie.
They are my daily cross, my whip, my yardstick, my score card.
The cruelest of the faithful,
the kindest of the cruel,
the lowliest of lowly things:
my _____ .

Solution: See answer page at back of book

The Test

A pessimist and optimist were best
of friends until the day a learnèd man
enlisted them as subjects in a test.
"Half empty or half full?" his question ran.
The two had shared a pint or glass of wine
and schmoozed for years, the wont of many men,
but never thought to analyze the stein
or criticize the glassware used, till then.

—Half full. —Half *empty!* —How the two friends fought,
and over nothing! —You're both working class? —
the doctor asked. And then the two friends, not
concerned about the status of the glass
but stricken by the smiling doctor's sneer,
in tandem, decked him, and went out for beer.

Yours?

There are mines
to mine,
and there are mines
that are mines.

Don't know if that's been
your experience,
but it's been
mine.

Test Markets

If Peace on Earth came in a little gizmo
that they could sell in one of those displays
near the cashier at a theme park's gift shop
with one sample assembled for your kids
to see so that they couldn't help but tug
at your sleeve and say Daddy Mommy look
can we get one can we can we can we
then everybody blithe enough to stop
at the gift shop would buy one like we buy
the rest of what we don't need. How we'd take
it home, since it won't settle in a box,
would be a problem, surely, and at next
spring cleaning, we'd be apt to throw it out.
But notwithstanding technicalities
like those, the larger problem is to get
the rest of us admission to the park
and time to browse like suckers in a store
and then of course to take the thing out of
the crate, assemble it, see how it works,
and if we can figure it out, then help
the rest of the world's theme park visitors
and impulse buyers (isn't everyone?)
assemble theirs. It shouldn't be too tough.

two

!!!

The Roar of Grass

The reason I do not indeed cannot
walk God's earth looking down at the adjustment
of my hand laden by a palm-sized plate
with lights and letters on it is that once
I heard the roar of grass and am convinced
that such a thing might happen yet again
even where there's no grass like in a store
or office tower elevator bank
or on a train or plane or boat or in
a crowd or some such seemingly ungreen site
which sure as hell I wouldn't want to miss
so I keep my eyes and ears held close and open
as it was on that August day with you
when we lay on the tickling grass and kept
one ear on it the other to the sky
and our eyes on each other and there was
such a roar

Full Service Staff

I do not want to think of you as vultures
on either side of dawn when I'm not dead
but only feel dead by the elevator.
And yet your uniforms *are* vulture-hued.
Nor do I want you thinking that I'm rude;
I'm just not ready, eyes still wet and red,
to answer quips like *How are you?* till later.

But it's the newest thing in modern cultures
for those-who-serve to need so much from those-
who-pay so much for cruises and hotels.
Smile, nod, stand tall—you can stand on your toes
to show us that you're there and there with bells
on. Chit-chat, though, comes off as merely mean
when souls are sore deficient in caffeine.

Flight of Knowledge

They have no sea to swim in.——Marina Zalesski

The things to know, they never knew, nor knew
they didn't know. So what were they to do
when crisis came? They had no sea to swim
in. When they had us, things were growing grim,
but no one knew they were. We swam on sand,
indulged, adored, well-fed. And it was grand
not knowing all there was to know about,
nor how to go about finding out.

How good we feel about ourselves still, though,
not knowing, and not knowing we don't know.

I have a dream, though, sometimes, of a sea
far from the sand's self-styled *democracy*
where schools are fearless: even guppies, taught
to navigate the wetter world of thought.
There, fins turn, every now and then, to wings
(as in the Escher print) from knowing things
like how to look within and how to look
without; or how to find an honest book
to help us see, at night, the light of day;
the Way to Know, or how to know the Way;

and not just look and think, but *that* we should;
that with true thought, there's nothing that we could
not do; and that no truly worthwhile thoughts
can be contained or cast in such dry dots

as we've been filling in on data sheets
for The Machine That Doesn't Read, but eats.

All makes sense in my dream!

                              And then I wake,
made blank once more, though with a plangent ache
all over, like a memory of yore
that Once Upon a Time we learned to soar.

Huey

When Long said *Every man's a king*
he made a lot of noise
but didn't tell us anything—
Just look at little boys:

At five they stand like lording lords;
at six they implement,
as generals and tyrants, words
they too seldom repent.

The bold lie is about as new
as bad boys' lame excuses;
the slogans, coined expressly to
encourage the abuses:

Boys will be boys, the fathers say;
the moms, *What can I do?*
while teachers turn the other way
and no one thinks to sue—

which victims could, but do not know.
So bullies once again
unruled remain unschooled and grow
into unruly men.

O listen to their armies' drums!
Beware the legions bossed

who'll bear the brunt of Kingdom-Come's
Apocalyptic cost!

Though platitude's a useful thing
when spun like children's toys,
the truth's not just that *men are kings*
but men and kings are boys.

Word Choice

Kindness suggests an act, that is, volition;
niceness—a trait, veneer, or a condition,
I think. So, noting the dexterity
of your teenage-like thumbs (that's if I dare
speak to you, a complete stranger to me,
on the lift, summoning you from elsewhere)
I'll praise your thumbs. You might respond, "Thank you."
(Ignoring folks, I find, I cannot do.)
If you, then, do not even seem to mind
my interruption of your concentration
but look up with a smile from your device
and even deign to make a conversation,
I'll part by saying, "Thanks for being nice,"
but think that you're most likely also kind.

Silk Worm

The silk worm struts in silence.

Struts, not slithers? you ask, aghast;

To which I ask, in turn,
Tell me, proud friend:

What empire is vaster and more regal
than the lowly silk worm's,

who dedicates himself only
to making others feel good

about themselves?

I met a modern man

I met a modern man one day
    who looked but could not see
the me in front of him for all
    the tags attached to me.

He noted I was someone of
    my height, weight, age and race.
And from my accent, he could tell
    that I'd come from some place.

Wanting to know how much I made,
    he asked me what I do
and how much that profession paid:
    I told him and he knew.

He took note of the model and
    the year of what I drive
and nodded at my home address
    when he asked me where I live.

I've met this man so often, friends
    have seen a change in me,
the onset of a rather quirksome
    personality.

Now, when I meet a modern man
    and he asks such-and-such,
I make up facts, then ask him, *Does
    it matter all that much?*

Δ

Whatever salary I make
  you are welcome to half;
and if you're homeless, my home's yours.
  When *homeless* gets a laugh—

he's never homeless—there is hope.
  Then I ask him a thing or two,
like favorite parks, and types of days.
  I like snow—what about you?

If by then he has not beaten
  the hastiest retreat
I might inquire, *Say have you eaten?*
  Let's go somewhere and eat!

And then I get that modern man
  to talk of other things
than things, like parks and snow and men
  who don't enjoy such things.

Then I pick up the check and treat
  so that he owes me one.
And it's up to him whether or not
  a friendship has begun.

My friends point out I can't afford
  to treat like this, but I'm
determined to give modern man
  a chance. And it saves time.

Looks

The birthing mother could not see.
    She needed the midwife
to bring to her the little face
    and show the little life
    that had just come to be

    till various improvements in
      the mirror let her look
directly, while the little face
emerged from her. But the improving took
too long. Meanwhile, a prototype of sin

had taken hold. For, long before,
    while scions breathed their first,
    dark spirits slipped inside the door,
      unseen (of course at night the room
was dimly lit, back then), went in the womb,
    and left their fingerprints.
And regardless of what you might believe,
    it looks like that may be why we've
        been
        cursed
      ever since.

My Pothos

Ever green and young, this plant
takes over anywhere in spite
of everything I do. I can't
decide if it prefers more light
and water or would rather less,
the way it sprawls no matter where
it's put: like teenage boys, I guess,
    who grow all the more, the less you seem to care.

Tips often blotch, bend, and turn brown
and yellow, but whenever I
pinch them off, even more fall down.
The whole plant, though, will never die,
for green shoots quickly take their place,
    as if they were part of a plan, or master race.

Priestess

A priestess never needed a black cat,
     nor, necessarily, a broom to fly,
nor sported warty nose and conic hat;
we have the Modern World to thank for that.
     Nor did she ever tout as her ally
the guy with hooves and horns in bright red dress.
     It was the Patriarch that made the switch
and changed the awe-some into an abscess,
and what was sacred, into ugliness
     herself, the holistic into a witch,
a crone, or at the very least, a crank.
     I was not nine yet saw something amiss
in those harsh demonizing ways, and thank
     Elizabeth Montgomery for this.

Posture

Two points define
a line
but also any man:
the point at which he cannot stop himself
and the point at which he can
not help but stop:
the latent criminal and the inner cop.

I've left these alter-egos on the shelf
deporting in the midst of moving men
and women like a noble citizen.
But the points, like instant seeds, I carry within,
the axis of a seeming rectitude.

The one I silence when I could be rude
and let the other laugh and imagine
the magnitude of an impending sin.

In other words, when I'm about to holler,
these two points stretch me, some, and I stand taller.

Achievement

Achievement does not always race for gold
to sport a wreath in a ring in front of a crowd,
but crawls, unnoticed, most times. He's not proud
but incognito, plodding along, bold
as small boys who persist in picking berries
in spite of losses to the belly and the ground;
or as ants, who start repairing formicaries
as soon as the rain's stopped, unsung as the sound
of silent partners, plucky as blue-stained boys,
who've little use for laudatory noise—
that's genius toiling. And when a machine
is able at last to pick the bushes clean,
the ant's unmoved, because he understands
Achievement's but a shifting of the sands.

the tamer

Mercurio's whip
crackles in use

turns limp when it is done
and deposed on the hook
where it belongs
where even now it is hung.

Between show and rehearsal
outside the cage
Mercurio's
a different animal.
When there are no more lions though
what will he be?

Pen-obsessed
I likewise ask
the gates to be unpinned.
Heaven forbid
that the creatures
have been tamed.

Critics

Critics live in others' lives
like arbiters in fates of wives.

Horse Man

By schooling him in stable rows he trains his colts to run by rote
and answer questions he will pose by hoofing it for hay or oat

while carrots hung before the snout keep asses pulling forth a plow
instead of looking all about (which worthy masters can't allow);

and intermittent sounds of cracks from whips of yet another Master
keep *him* circling racing tracks and coursing ever farther, faster.

The fact the Master's missing, and that there's no driver in the seat
is something he can't understand so he, too, plies with equine feet

and the momentum of the race stirs up the breeze that keeps in place
the blinders so they frame his face as long as he keeps up the pace.

And yet were he to take a pause the flaps would fall and free his eyes
which with a little exercise could lead him right, left, up or down,

to open fields, or into town where he could stand up like a man.
Oh, help the Horse Man if you can!

But blind faith in a noble cause contents a beast to stay the course
(as if commanded by a Book) and never stop and take a look
but, for the Master, go full force

around and around and around and stay the horse.

Sudden summer rains

Sudden summer rains
Trap, surprise, refresh, cool, dry—
What a balm for minds!

Mad. Man

There is a Mad. Man still behind the curtain
pushing buttons, pulling string after string,
adjusting dials that don't do anything
but make demands through smoke, reverb, and a
dismembered head. The only thing that's certain
is that although exposed the process will
continue in the Marvelous Land of Awe,
so vast that only glitter dreams can fill
it with products that prettify the face
or drape the walking dead to seem less mad
and help us land a spot on Melrose Place,
plus other wondrous things I wish I had:
a heart, a home, the nerve, a bit of brain,
and the power to purchase them again and again.

The Great Party

In last night's dream I was five years old again
And went to a friend's sixth birthday party.
 At the end of musical chairs, a game
  We all already knew well how to win,
   The mother frowned and told the winning boy,
    "I'm so sorry,"
     Then kissed him on the forehead, shook her head,
      Kissed each of us in turn, as if we all
       Had boo-boos on our heads. "Perhaps next year,"
       She said,
        "You will do better." We had our cookies and cake,
         Then yielded our presents, laughing through sugary grins.

       When next year came around—we were still five,
        As if a spell kept us from turning six—
         We won and failed, were kissed and crammed and gave
          Again. Well, after many years of this,
           We started growing wary of never growing up.

        This last time, though, last night, before the music stopped,
         I turned to my circling neighbor, had a new thought, and said,
         "No you sit down."

       That little girl—to whom I gave the chair—
        Turned to me and looked awfully relieved
        Not to be the first to fail and lose.
       And that made me happy, and I told her so.
       About to sit, she turned to the next boy:
       "No *you* sit down."
       "No *you*."

"No *you*."
And all of us
At that great party would not sit until
We hunted through the house for one more seat.
There'd been plenty of chairs for everyone all along!
And in a flash we turned into
Adults.

Forgiving

You know what Hindus say: that we return
to make up for this life's ills and abuses;
the Western model, that we either burn,
or wait to move. So if the State of Grace is
the Kingdom of God toward which we strive,
it's coming, but seems never to arrive.

But other realms are worth the founding: To
Forgive, for one. Yourself as well as others.
Then, not need to, because the person you
become sees neighbors as sisters and brothers—
and, when the realm's frontiers swell to the seas,
not only neighbors but your enemies.

For that family comprises givers, takers,
bullies, victims, heroes who are hitters,
good-deed-doers who are really fakers,
the shat upon (forgive me) and the shitters;
those who are miserable—for no real reason,
their earthly circumstances being blessed
with riches—, neither moved by nor impressed,
if they even note, the changing of a season.

You've known——? Well I have been all the above,
forgave myself, then you, then learned to love
in such a way I don't need to forgive
so much now. It's as hard to understand
as to explain—like living in a land
remote from everything that I once was,

that coexists in the same continuum
of time and space, accessible because
you can leave the world of Was and Will—for Am,
the Kingdom that comes even while we live.

Blossoms

For all their beauty, blossoms have no heart:
Nor eyes, so do not share the beauty of
Their fellow blooms. But though no flower love,
Neither can it feel lonely or apart
For, with no brain to think, it cannot know
Of its or others' singularity.

Some flowers branch from others, visibly
Joined at a common stem, the way they grow;
Others share common roots beneath the soil:
But even these sprout independent blooms
Disjoint from all neighbors, save for the toil
Of picking, gathering, bunching a bouquet;

Or reallotting nectars into combs
Of honey, to partake, as poetry.

How You Know

How do you know there's love?

I'll tell you how you know there's love.

Love is there when turning to each other you turn into each
other too.

Think about loving your dog or cat: the frolicking mew or ruff
on the ground in a welter of beast and you; the lift and the
purr or the pant blobbing up to your shoulder; your ear,
lapped and drenched with loving goop, if not devoured.

Think of your favorite peanut butter stuck to the ceiling of your
mouth so that when you were asked a question suddenly
your voice was the voice of peanut butter itself: the viscous,
delicious, inscrutable ooze you love even to this day.

And think of your love, not of creatures or things, but of doing:
hiking, climbing, jogging, swimming, biking, playing. You
become not the trail or the hill or the road or the pool or
the pond or the sea or the game, but
hiking, climbing, jogging, swimming, biking, playing itself. So
that in France, you jumped in the Mediterranean, scaled
three alps, and pedaled from château to château to château.
Well, I did, anyway.
Substitute what *you* do, and cannot help but do, and you'll
know there is love.

And now that you've gotten this far, that we've gotten this far
together, and you've digested the above—and why else

would you have kept on to here?——then I am where you are,
    which is here. And part of me, this part of me
is rolling in your mind, and is part of you; the turn to each
    other has turned us into ourselves; outward is inward; two
    are miraculously one.

And you know.

three

. . .

The Arbitrary

One turning point's
The point of middle age
The arbitrary point of realization
That you're half way to where you don't want to be.

A second point's
The point of mellow wisdom
An arbitrary time you realize
If you have the time
And inclination to go around realizing things
That from the slap on your bottom in the delivery room
Way back when
You started dying as you started living.

They are the same thing, the same activity,
Two sides of the same coin, and only words.
Thenceforth all days are delivered
Fleeting as they are precious,
Precious as fleeting.

And middle age and old age are just terms
Of arbitrary concepts.

Although this second, arbitrary point,
Like all wisdom, depending on when it comes,
Rarely comforts, barely reassures.

The Ride

Face backwards and you see your wake,
almost on its creation,
dissolve. Or see cross currents break
it up. Imagination
works like this. What you've just now thought
is like the boated lake,
so many patterns drawn, and there, then not.

Face frontward. Now what do you see?
Conjecture. Tricks of the mind.
The future, fingered. Tributary
here, there—options left behind
once you proceed. What was and is
traded for what will be.
Will and caprice, a trading business.

Because most mornings I will find
a mist where I have been,
and every evening, darkness will
obscure where I will go,
I find the moment I am in
will curiously remind
me of how little that I know.
It's a bit like being still.
Or riding blind.

Riddle 4

Every second, every day, she nears.
Upon arrival, though, she disappears—
Or, more accurately stated, moves away,
Still chased, while chaste yet, for another day.

Solution: See answer page at back of book

"Made Thing"

1.

I wanted to be Good and did some Thing
thought Good, but later learned that it was Wrong—
worse, Bad. The gods wreaked vengeance. But I'd sing
of the fiasco in a stupid song

I wrote, and thought that I could be happy
through song. But then I learned that any word
I chose got misconstrued invariably
for its inverse—or, worse, was never heard.

The gods guffawed. What gods, you ask: those of
my making, who would have me miserable,
if worthwhile: have me love but need no love,
only to suffer some Thing to feel full,
only to offer some Thing made as new,
as if it mattered, like a love, to you.

2.

If Goodness is a Martinet
and Happiness a Goblin
then Worthiness can only be
an intrepid Pioneer—
who, even hapless, must be free
to disobey the Martinet,

and play deaf to the Goblin
        to forge on to the next frontier.

And all three dwell where Ego lives.
The four at constant war in me,
they summon representatives
who draft the occasional treaty
        that peace be sought and found, in poetry.

3.

Is peace enough? I cannot say.
But in this peace there lies
endurance, day to night to day,
as any Carpenter applies
His soft skills to make things that hold
great meals, small lanterns, urns of gold . . .
        around which souls may sup, or read, or pray.

Sodden Song

'The ocean
'zthe solution,'
slurred the seaman
in devotion
to the notion
of the ocean
as the potion
and the lotion
of his life
which in truth
years ago
in his youth
we all know
it had been.
Now he lives alone
and there's none for folks to phone
so out blurts his sodden song—

'I've done the whole thing wrong!
The story of my life,
my poor mistreated wife,
three sons that I don't see,
no, they never knew me.
Now look at what I got.
Wooja pour another shot?
I wazjh in the na-vee.
That wazjh the life — the sea.

But WhaddI come to be?
I've done the whole thing wrong. . .'

Well by now that sodden song
had got a little long.
When the slim bartender,
not quite blameless for the bender,
tisked his tongue and shook his head,
the old tar's younger buddy said,
'But then you wouldn't be
here with me!'
Then the tar full of devotion
to the potion (and the ocean)
burped 'n' laughed, 'That's right,
Buddy, abso-tively right!
Now lookie what I've got.
Hey, how 'bout another shot?'

But Buddy, with a wink
to the barman, quashed the drink
to the tar-man on the brink
of oblivion. 'I think,'
Buddy said, 'it would be sweet
if we got something to eat.'
Then he got him off his seat
and helped him to his feet,
so the two of them could beat,
well, an *un*hasty retreat.
They made it to the car,
but they hadn't gotten far

when the erstwhile tar
started reminiscing
about sea lives they were missing
and he promised his new friend
he'd shtay wizzum till the end
of the war, and never
would forget, not ever,
how they'd saved each other's lives
and introduced each other's wives.
'I will nivver forget...'
But of course he was all wet.
With a belch and a cough
he nodded off.

So Buddy drove him home,
wiped the froth and foam
from his passenger's chin.
Then he carried him in,
and kissed him to bed
and softly said,
sort of sodden, sort of sad,
'So. Then. All right.
G'night, . . .
Dad.'

Imaginary Options

One option is: Cut down the "man" who did it
as you have dreamt of, so you could feel better.
But would you? Or show everyone the letter
that cousin wrote you back, proud to admit it
in writing. Sue for damages and use
his own words, notwithstanding that his phrase
you liked it will give other cousins pause
when you have kept it in for all your days
since you were

                  twelve. I don't know what advice
I can give you today so that you can,
tomorrow, live, if we can call it "live."
To kill a killer won't make you a man,
but only let the killer kill you twice....

I'll do it for you, Dad. I am not twelve.

clothes weep in the dryer

clothes weep in the dryer
lint tears I (with love) remove
restored, slightly less

Spoon and Dish

Should you have laughed so at the cruel sport?

Should I have overleapt the horny moon?

And what about the *other* dish and spoon,
the ones abandoned that night (on a shelf
and in a drawer, respectively) to sort
the mess out and go on with damaged lives?

Does what they did remind you of yourself?

At first they dated other dishes, knives
and forks, but, while attractive in their shine,
these tended to lie, slice, or even pierce.

In time, though, Spoon and Dish met, became friends,
and grew to trust each other with a fine
and lasting love.

Their exes, playing fierce
and fast, twice more divorced, met violent ends.

Look

You left to have a look within yourself, you said, without
me getting in the way. I took you at your word. I doubt
you can imagine how it felt, to be alone again.
I hoped that you would have a good look and be back. But
    When?,
I asked myself, over and over, learning to survive
without the least idea of why you'd left, or I'm alive,
other than that when you'd told me I never looked within,
just outward—that that's who I'd always be, and always been—

you must have been correct. And that "the gap between us" was
too deep, too wide, to ever be traversed, because—. Because.
And last night, on the avenue, while seeing you was sweet,
I don't think that it crossed my mind, when I crossed the street,
that you would either have to cross as well, or have to shout
my name to bridge the distance. I was just—looking out.

Mustard

Mustard
can't be flustered.
Yet no one dreads its sting.
In fact it is expected
to taste interesting.

Custard
unlike mustard
is innocent and light
and usually confected
expressly not to bite.

Now you think I am custard,
    but you don't understand
it's only my good breeding
    that makes you think I'm bland.

For I am really mustard
    and would go well with ham.
Put down what you are reading
    and you'll see that I am.

Hephaestus at the Forge Shows his Back Room

Be careful, though, I wouldn't want to burn
you. It's a little cooler in the back
but let me shower first, I'm turning black
from all the soot. Yeah, that's the Grecian urn
they wrote up, once. I'll shower fast. My cot
is big, I work late all the time, that's life.
At least I have a job. My wife? My wife
is out of town. She's out of town a lot.

It's comfortable here, and never cold.
Besides at home once I reached out to hold
her in the middle of the night, and it
got chilly fast. Yeah, she was in the city,
      overnight. I curse her business trips
but sure am glad you use her beauty tips.

Venus and Vulcan

If she's the avatar of Love *and* Beauty
then tell me why She screws around with hearts.
And what divine or morbid sense of duty
keeps Her supplyin' Cupid with those darts?
And what's She doin' hangin' round with War
all night? You would expect that from a God,
but if such lightness is what She stands for,
what's to distinguish Venus from a bawd?

And hubby Vulcan, poundin' at His forge
all day and all night, bang bang bang bang. He's
no time to exercise His pressin' urge
for Her. So if you count fidelity,
Vulcan's the God of Work *and* Love, while She's
a planet, plus the root of a disease.

How True Love Lies

after John Donne, done after

At first sight,
            through Invention;
on speaking,
            soft Impression;
at a touch,
            Anticipation;
only lying,
            Consummation.

*

Should you love back months or more,
I may mutter
            I Love You,
I Have Never Loved Before,
                        or
that
      This Love Is True.

*

With so many lying stages,
"true love" (it would seem) must be
an oxymoron for the ages,
you,
      my love,
            and me.

*

Like the parables of Zen,
though,
          some truth may lie in it.
Let us lie together, then,
ohh,
     at least another minute.

Proofs

I had this friend I used to gad about
with in moot mathematical adventures
wherein we'd churn excitement out of doubt
by systematically working proofs out
to evidence the most far-fetched conjectures:

We'd show we were not really here, yet were;
that points existed QED, and not.
But I liked woods and hills, and would adjure
him to join me there. This he would refer
to as 'treason.' I had a favorite spot

in the hills where I often went to lose
myself in the green rapture of a day's
hike, in the peaceful transport of its views.
There I made new friends, since he would refuse
to come. At last we went our separate ways.

Years later in the Home Town News I read
his body had been found below the high
cliff of a mountain ravine, smashed and dead.
A freakish hiking accident, it said.
And we all said What a sad way to die

at the wake. His sister took me aside.
She knew I'd known that promontory well
and said, 'He went in search, before he died,

of what he said you'd found there.' Then she cried
a bit, but she had more to show and tell:

She eked a smile and handed me, from him,
a pair of hiking boots, almost brand new,
recovered (later) up at the cliff's rim.
They had been placed there with this note: For Jim.
He'd remembered we wore the same size shoe.

Leap of Love

He teetered at a precipice,
our class clown, to impress a miss.
She would not look, which had him stumped:

> finally he jumped.

In love
    "until my dying day,"
a few of us had heard him say—

> we knew he never lied.

Perhaps she heard him as he cried
her name while dancing off the rim

> and every now and then will think of

him.

Condolences 2

My heart goes to the family of the dead. (And to the dying.)
But how he took our breath away risking all by driving
without a safety belt. (Once, twice—well, once too often,
     surely,
the last time being his last race as you know—which he nearly
won, didn't he? What happened was, they'd changed the
     regulation,
but he did not adhere because it was not his tradition,
I guess, to fasten the safety belt. So he sped round and round,
and crashed. And oh the loss we felt when his body was found.

Some call him hero. I can't say that word, for had he fastened
his, he'd still be alive today. But who has ever listened
to common sense, or what's not said, certainly not Dale Senior,
so why his fans, now that he's dead? No, let us root for Junior,
a hero if sports ever had one. How the bleachers rise
to cheer him on and go half-mad and buy his merchandise.)

R. I. P. Dale Earnhardt, 1951-2001

even / a red tear

even
a red tear
will dry

Thetis

O women of the world, of course you are
the envy of the other half of man,
for we're but half, and not blessed with the power
    to bear a child the way you can.

There is a goddess in you, every one.
And should you come upon the River Styx
(or its equivalent), you'd dip your son
    too so he'd get through any fix

in later life. But Mothers, will you shy
to get your hands wet with the ghoulish waters
and leave one ankle, where you hold him, dry?
    Will you do the same with your daughters?

Remember, once he's gone outside the womb,
you've given him two ankles and two feet.
Thetis dunked once, which sealed Achilles' doom;
    You?—*please* switch ankles, and repeat.

Ariadne

Remember, if you've come upon this note
    And wish to work the maze to claim the prize,
That there's a monster girded by this moat
    Who's slain about a hundred other guys.

But if you will not fight, and even die
    For me, although I much prefer you kill,
Then I would just as soon you pass me by—
    But pass this on to someone else who will.

Last from the Past

The "Last Civil War Veteran" came
at the end of a long day
clad in faded taupe or slate.
He spoke about the fray—
campaigns, generals, blood and deaths—
in a quiet way.

No one asked which side he'd fought for,
the Blue or the Gray;
he barely whispered *us* and *them*,
so none of us could say.
Next day, we began wondering if
not knowing was OK.

Cemetery Patterns

We'll take the Ant Hill.
—Kirk Douglas in Stanley Kubrick's film *Paths of Glory*

The paths of glory lead but to the grave.
—Thomas Gray

I do not think they understood what *paths*
of glory meant when charging up their hill.
These spans of soldiers are but aftermaths
of hero-journeys through the birth canal.
True glory lies, though, and lies with the mother.
Her powers, no son ever gains. Her plaques
and medals, he can't win, and so attacks
in angered enterprises for another.

Not understanding such a subtle thing,
my cemetery soldier underlies
it as I lie beneath these steel-cold skies
and cronish myrtles, dormant, numb, mourning
till night annuls the light that days evince
and, wondering on his star, I wish, then wince.

By Graveyards

When riding by a graveyard with Ashley,
who's known for wit and slows down and applauds,
I also clap, in case some soul might be
in need of commendation to the gods.

When walking through a graveyard, though, alone
to gather in the quiet, or with others,
I have been known to pause and stroke a stone,
especially a small child's, a young mother's.

When joining in to clap as Ashley claps,
by graveyards, my hands have a way of staying
together—for applause, too long, perhaps:
Once Ashley said he thought he caught me praying.

How and Where

When Mr. F was taken down
his sons tried not to cry.
    He'd been depressed
    but neither guessed
that he'd decide to die.

O why not choose some distant town,
and potion, of some kind?
    Why undress
    and leave a mess
for family to find?

It's one thing to decide to act;
another, *how* you do it;
    a third is *where*.
    So why not spare
your loved ones, and think through it?

Any poison can in fact
effect the same grim crime—
    or motel room,
    a final doom
before your slotted time.

Unless, like F, a gory death
is what you're also wanting
    with screams and tears

and harried years
of hurt and harm and haunting . . .

For that's what F gave Mrs. F
and both his sons, still living:
    three lives of hell
    (I know them well):
the gift that won't stop giving.

After a Calamity

You keep busy. At least you are doing something positive.

You keep busy. At least you are doing something

You keep busy. At least you are doing

You keep busy. At least you are

You keep busy. At least you

You keep busy at least

You keep busy at

You keep busy

You keep

You

after Judy Blume

On Turning Adversity into Art

Lose?—

Blues!

Tattoo

A tattoo is a superficial thing
in a likewise world. But it is always there,
unlike most other things that make no sense.
And it is only superficial on
the surface, for it's commemorating
some image or event that made you care
enough, even if in your ignorance
or youth, or drunk with friends one weary dawn,
to mark yourself in perpetuity
not as you were but as you chose to be.

The old man who has lost old friends, ex-wives
and children to their more exotic lives,
might not have much that's his, or much to do,
but one thing that's still his is his tattoo.

Whether or Not

The morning thrush and lark, which greet the dawn
or make it, sing no matter who is there
to hear. When that resilience is gone
and nature herself starts to disappear

another Coming will be under way
where souls of things and beings shall impart
new traits to old forms to attend the day-
song; air shall grow ears; soil, assume a heart;

tongues, noses, fingertips and eyes shall be
affixed to blades, leaves, lakes, florescences,
clouds, mist: that all, in all humility,
shall listen, taste, feel, savor all that is
and its anthem, the morning call of birds,
long after you and I are gone, and words.

Shadows 1

I met you in the shadows
smitten by a lust
which I construed as caring, or at least a basic trust.

But in the dark, a rainbow
appeared: all differences,
like bands, bent, tightly bound by human magic—glorious.

And in the light, the meadow
you took me to, to lay
in flowers, grass and you, made equal magic of the day.

Then I went through a window
as complications grew
from being with, well, darling, it could only have been you.

And now we meet as shadows.
Once more, I almost live.
Now tell me: when did you find out that you were Positive?

1985

The phone rang weekly in that early age
of ringing, wringing out ammonia tears,
when the plague was new. Actors of too few years
and roles were lost, too many ghosts of stage
and film too quickly made. Now, calls from lover,
spouse or sibling are rarer, but not over.

Were you to phone today and tell me that
you'd found my number starred beside my name
in his black book, and thought that you should take
the time to dial me up and tell me what
he'd thought of me, that I was not the same
as others he'd known, I'd ask *When's the wake?*
and tell you to be glad that you're alive.

I might not have, in 1985.

My Marker

If a tree, when I am gone, grew over my grave
instead of a planted stone, which cannot grow,
it would serve as my marker only as long
as the life of, and shadow cast by, the loyal tree.

But the stone (already ordered, by the way)
will only serve effectively as long
as someone comes to read it, drop a flower,
or walk a dog to sniff and drop a gift.

Thank you, O unmet opener of this,
for reading up to here. The words may be
ephemera today, but were first scratched
on paper pulped and pressed from a stalwart tree
purposed if not for immortality
at least for a remarked longevity.

after Saigyó

Meeting of the Minds

I don't want to abuse you or misplace you
but in your distance can't help but create you
even though I would much rather face you
not the you I've created which of late you
have become for me. Do you know that this you
has all of you plus parts that may not be you
but you inspire? With this you I don't miss you
nearly as much as when I do not see you.

It's on invention then that I rely,
pumped by this heart (your heart)'s pathetic beat
which triggers this imaginative mind
to otherwise imagine. If this I
be your invention, in it you will find
all of me and more, were we to meet.

Syzygy and Triangle

I saw Buckminster Fuller demonstrate
(with Tinker Toys®) the endurance of the tri-
angle, its firm form unadultered by

shaking or waving, and how it bore weight
better than any square or beam-and-lin-
tel. But we three aren't dowels joined at in-

tersections with pre-manufactured holes.
With our alignment, one of us must lie
in the middle. Were we but loving souls,

not two planets bound to a hungry star
between, in a celestial syzygy,
lasting a moment, you and you and me,

Time—and Motion, her dresser—would not be
the ravager of this, the enemy
of Us. Notwithstanding that what we are

is heaven, and I love you equally,
as I know you, as you have said, love me
and each other: but this is for now;

I would that it could last, but don't know how,
other than in this note, left, that one day
some future race might read, and point the way.

Authorship

A little like a vampire: I would make
the dead eternal, and might seek a youth
to mesmerize awhile, or sink a tooth
into to make an acolyte——of some-
one like you, if you have the thirst to slake.

One day years hence a slew of you will come
with a crow upon my crypt. And as you pry
open my lid, I'll score a creaking sound,
with viol ostinato echoing round
my chamber of secrets tucked in the tome;

throw in a mad coyote in the distance
to test your nerve while draining your resistance.
Should we succeed, though, I'll not drink you dry,
but make your veins a vessel of the dead
by offering my blood to you, instead.

turning

Take the problem, the crystal enigma
you've flipped but cannot make heads or tails of.
Hold it firm and turn it upside down
and in the inversion, catch a lucky glimpse.
The facets right themselves, a sudden sense
or order in the chaos becomes clear.
And you can name it, solve it, readjust
it so its natural use as a prism
emerges. If you're lucky. If it was a prism.

If it is too big and heavy, though,
to be held and turned, then try to turn yourself.
Stand on your head, circle left three times
or circle it, if there's room, climb on top, crawl beneath,
if no room, at least stay awhile and blink—.
Do what you can, that is (except give in),
to see, and you shall see. I did, I think.

I have known people in this problemed life
who have shown me this process. I did not
know if they were lucky or if they were cursed
with being different. Then I'd catch a glimpse
of them through an inversion, found them kind,
and through their crystal enigmatic eyes,
their lives of process, ordering their crises
and chaos, and as quietly as dawn,

I've felt I too can turn into anything
and seen them for the prisms that they are.

The glass wall you perceive composes me
is made of flesh, experience and blood,
plus many revolutions of reflection
reglazed in suns and times. There's not one wall
but many. Blink. Turn. Move behind,
beneath, upon, . . . hold me in your hands
and shake me, if you will—at the very least, stay
awhile to enjoy the properties of the glass.
It's smooth and cools. And if you're lucky, you
might glimpse—as I did back when I was you—
a bit of everything, that you can turn
to anything, even to what you are.

Balm of Innocence

When I come back I'll come back as a tear
on the cold cheek of a sensitive gray maid
to salve the once-soft skin now growing sere
where good men's tepid lips have been indelibly delayed.

The next time I come back I'll find the face
of a birthday boy whose sporty father's gone;
I'll wait with him beneath the dark staircase
till midnight by the front door and the aching, unrung phone.

Right now, though, it's your stillness I accept,
your silent howl, for I have come to lend
an ear if not the tear you sorely lack,
the balm of innocents. Or, if you've slept
horrendously and do not want a friend
just yet, I'll go. Then later, if you wish, I'll come back.

Before Language

Because there is language
we have the word Here.
And because there is Here,
There.
Which may be what I can see that's not Here,
what is by you, not by me:
or what is by neither of us
but can also be beyond all I see:
Imagination.

But once upon a time, before language,
there was no here and there,
nor now and then,
nor you and I,
only us
as ever
as one.

And when we are silent
together
I start
to remember
a time
like that—
or, rather,
like this—
or both,
as ever,
as one.

Trip of a Lifetime

The place within.
Shall we begin?

Turns & Twists

Acknowledgments

Thank you to my friend Randi Sobol for looking at this collection a few times and helping me figure out what it wanted to be all along.

Also, grateful acknowledgment is made to the editors of the following periodicals and web-sites where poems first appeared:

Alabama Literary Review: "Forgiving"; *The Aurorean:* "My Marker"; *Barrow Street:* "By Graveyards"; *Better Than Starbucks:* "clothes weep in the dryer" and *"Sudden summer rains";* *Binnacle:* "Blossoms" and "Condolences 2"; *Blue Collar Review:* "Huey"; *Blue Unicorn:* "Doppelganger"; *Bluepepper:* "The Shortest Distance"; *Book XI:* "Genesis"; *Calliope* (Mensa): "Figurative"; *Clackamas Literary Review:* "Look"; *Cold Mountain Review:* "I met a modern man"; *Contemporary Rhyme* and *Circe's Cauldron* (Bibliotheca Alexandrina): "Priestess"; *Cortland Review:* "The Gate"; *Decadent Review:* "How True Love Lies"; *The Delinquent:* "even / a red tear"; *Descant* (TCU): "The Roar of Grass"; *Empty Sink Publishing:* "turning"; *enskyment* (anthology, Moon Shadow Sanctuary Press): "Full Service Staff"; *erbacce:* "Imaginary Options"; *Fickle Muses:* "Ariadne"; *Frogmore Papers:* "Test Markets"; *Good Life Literary Journal:* "Silk Worm"; *Gravitas:* "Balm of Innocence"; *Green Silk Journal:* "Flight of Knowledge"; *Harnessing Fire: A Devotional Anthology in Honor of Hephaestus* (Bibliotheca Alexandrina): "Hephaestus at the Forge Shows his Back Room"; *Harvests of the New Millennium:* "Cemetery Patterns"; *Home Planet*

News: "Five Things That Can't Be Proved," "How You Know," and "V"; *Illuminations:* "At a Mirror"; *In Parentheses:* "The Existence of Two" and "Urban Adjustments"; *Ken*again:* "Math, Defender of the Faith" and "the tamer"; *Lily Poetry Review:* "Last from the Past"; *Literary Hatchet:* "Horse Man" and "product"; *Lord of the Horizon: A Devotional Anthology in Honor of Horus* (Bibliotheca Alexandrina): "Round the Corner"; *The Lyric:* "My Pothos"; *Manhattan Plaza* (WordTech), *Ladowich:* "1985"; *mgversion2>datura:* "Probability" and "The Test"; *Möbius:* "The Great Party"; *Moon Hollow Review:* "Looks"; *Muddy River Poetry Review:* "Before Language"; *New Writer:* "Syzygy and Triangle"; *Orbis:* "Construct"; *Ovunque Siamo:* "Which Comes First?"; *Parody:* "Sway"; *Pirene's Fountain:* "Sodden Song"; *Poem:* ' "Made Thing" ' and "The Ride"; *Poetry East:* "Endings"; *Raintown Review:* "Proofs"; *Rat's Ass Review:* "Posture"; *Raven Chronicles:* "Tattoo"; *Red Claw Press:* "The Process of Sleep"; *Society of Classical Poets:* "Generations," "Trip of a Lifetime," and "Riddle 4"; *Stickman Review:* "Mad. Man" and "Spoon and Dish"; *Stray Branch:* "How and Where"; *Sunken Lines:* "Mustard"; *Toe Good:* "Leap of Love"; *Trinacria:* "Paradox"; *US 1 Worksheets:* "After a Calamity"; *Verse Wisconsin:* "Cloud"; *Westward Quarterly:* "Sides"; *Wild Violet:* "Whether or Not"; *Wilderness House Literary Review:* "Coil"; *Wingless Dreamer Publisher:* "Authorship"; *With an Adamantine Sickle: A Devotional for the Titans* (Bibliotheca Alexandrina): "Thetis"; *Wordland:* "Shadows 1"; *Writers Haven:* "Achievement"

Answers to Riddles

Read every other letter starting with the second

Riddle 1 (pp 4-5) : acb hca dne gfe

Generations (pp 28-29) : qpg hno mnd ers

Riddle Using *They* & *Them* (p. 42) : fsg cha ilj eks

Riddle 4 (p. 81): stn olm nop rpr movw